The Route to Cacharel

The Route to Cacharel

Matthew C. Nickel

Five Oaks Press
FIVE-OAKS-PRESS.COM

Published by Five Oaks Press
Newburgh, NY 12550
five-oaks-press.com
editor@five-oaks-press.com

Copyright © 2016 by Matthew C. Nickel.
All rights reserved. First edition.

ISBN: 978-1-944355-90-6

Cover Art: Yves Brayer (1907-1990), Les Saintes-Maries-de-la-Mer, 1956, Oil on canvas 54x65cm, © 2016 Artists Rights Society (ARS), New York / ADAGP, Paris

Some of these poems first appeared in *Shawangunk Review*, *Des Hymnagistes: An Anthology*, and *Maple Leaf Rag IV*. The majority of the poems are here published for the first time.

Printed in the United States of America

*This book is for
Stoney & Sparrow*

Contents

I

Les Huîtres de Les Moutiers-en-Retz	5
Hunting the Ardennes with Colonel Cantwell	7
Le Grand Cerf et l'Ombre	9
A Good Clean Village—War Monument	10
Midnight Call from Normandy	12
La Pomme d'Eve	15
An Original Sin Image	17
Portraite d'Une Sainte	21
The Slow Deliberate Form of Affection	22
Hiking up Mutspitze with Hemingway and Pound	26
La Route de Cacharel	30
Poem for Denys Colomb de Daunant	34

II

Nekuia: Calling the Still Small Voice	
I. Roncevaux	39
II. Saint-Guilhem-le-Désert	42
III. Sainte-Baume	44
IV. Les Saintes-Maries-de-la-Mer	47
Coda—Le Pèlerinage	51

III

Not Just *La Patria*—For RPW	55
Notes for the Last Waltz	57
Waiting for Beatrice in the Alyscamps	60
Eau d'Eden: Farewell to Cacharel	62

*Blessèd sister, holy mother, spirit of the fountain, spirit of the garden
Suffer us not to mock ourselves with falsehood*

T. S. Eliot, "Ash Wednesday"

Yea, the darkness hideth not from thee; but the night shineth as the day: the darkness and the light are both alike to thee.

Psalm 139: 12

I

Les Huîtres de Les Moutiers-en-Retz

For Sparrow

If you could catch the myriad sweet wave-spray
ocean's gift compact like whitecap contractions

buy all forgotten houses salt-weathered along shore-roads
(rescue all lone artists selling salt cellars in Breton accents)

and kiss the wrinkled hands of sailors, ancient mariners,
who cross beyond the wind-stricken *gois*

you might find a certain sweeping loneliness
that satisfies all longing sought in drunken evenings

lost somewhere south or in Louisiana.
If I could taste once more that cold metallic

sharp and sea juice, no horseradish
Tabasco eye-burning, not even

mignonette with shallots tongue-squinting
just the *eau de vie* and oyster muscle

like the sea's heart on a scoop-shaped shell
nothing except ice and salt spray

and a cool white wine from the Vendée,
I could remember the water of life

the cleaning wind-waltz that walking winding roads
recalls beside sea exposed cows grazing

salt-marshes that color the sharp metallic
sky in shades far deeper than memory.

If we could hold that moment once more together—
like in a chorus as the audience sings

aloud in joyous longing—
where the green earth meets the distant blue

in a sparrow's song releasing us from
sacrifice at the water's edge

restrained only from seeking the drowned road to
Noirmoutier, raiding a dusk to this longing,

we might contain Time again
like that windy afternoon in July 2008

when we celebrated the wind's revolt
and *royalistes* martyred in open resistance

paused to drink their bitter cups by salt waters
and lantern shrines to sailors lost at sea, when

we prayed to the wind while casting shredded
cloths like offerings, like Saint Francis blessing

raging waves and wind gusts, a singular prayer
for release to the mystical oysters of Les Moutiers.

Hunting the Ardennes with Colonel Cantwell

Toward the end, he remembered the way the forest
looked and scrub oak, pines, the heather
smell under boots and wind in trees approaching
the mystery of the Siegfried Line, ominous
westwall in the early fall before the terror
of tree bursts and Hürtgen, the horror after.

And Hemingway described that forest like
an illustration for Grimm's Fairy Tales
that one with crows hovering above branches
looking for a sign of death at the crossroads;
a broken knight with no woman, no hound,
just a horn sound wing-flap and the *cauchemar*

Charlemagne dreamt, of the long breath,
the battle at Roncevaux, Roland's death
and the birth of the Holy Roman Empire:
what great things we make that we never get to tell
those who have gone before us, but having gone
help us make those great things each day.

I wish I could have brought Cantwell back
through the frozen lagoon and listened to his story
about the Ardennes, I wish I could have broken
the ice toward Beatrice hoisting the sun on
Santa Maria Assunta, watch Saint Hubert
hauling nets with old fishermen, Torcello boys,

on our way to Cipriani's for a Gordons—then find
Hemingway as the light strikes the tower on Torcello
and gathers the gold around Our Lady, the one mosaic

on Torcello about which Hemingway felt *no doubt*.
Maybe Cantwell found his cure for the dark night
in Renata's love, maybe he felt *no doubt* as he

wondered about getting Christian toward the end—
but what really matters is the way we listen
with infinite love and compassion to the broken soldier
who needs to tell one more story before he dies
about hunting the enemy in mystical landscape
and finding in mystery a moment of grace.

Le Grand Cerf et l'Ombre

After E. P.

The old stag stands in the forest
The spirit of the stag drifts in the half-light filtered
           through
              beech leaves and crossed antlers

Le Grand Cerf glides in the sun-crossed shaking sweet fern. . . .

As light as the shadow of the leaves
           that shape the fern and forest floor
He moved among cathedral pews
Praying he walked with patches of stained light upon him

Domine, non sum dignus, the prayer still on his tongue
"Help thou thy unbelief"
And he: "that ship?
And two seas I've abided over."
"Not so far, no, not so far now,
There is an island—where no one knows—
A land fairer than day . . ."
                "*Nunc dimittis servum tuum,*
Domine, secundum verbum tuum in pace."

He prays the sign,
        thinking

Large as the shadow of the stag
That waits for the arrow in the green dark forest.

A Good Clean Village—War Monument

Gorge du Tarn, France

To have gone off and left the gorge
Deeply cut with river flowing,
To have gone off and watched them die
One by one, into the trenches

Friends, cousins, the man who gave you
A wooden cross for Noël, the cousin
Who taught you to swim, Uncle Jacques
Who held stained hands around yours,

Holding the taut line jerked by trout
Fighting in the green swollen river
Icy around shivering thighs,
Satisfactory holding in the current,

To have gone off to watch your brother
Bleed to death in the mud beside you
Your father caught by Germans, witness to
His execution, one pistol to the head

One shot you did not hear for the screaming
Breath dry in your mouth as you ran
Toward them caught by your mother's brother
Thrown down to save you from yourself,

To have gone off and to walk back, alone
To the gorge wind and moving stream, to the
High pass and cliff clutch, to the nothing
That crumbles from the limestone edges

To have gone off and to come back
Arched shoulders burdened
All for a German tourist loud with camera
Taking your picture unaware

As you wash your lettuce in the branch
That cuts the village, where you used to
Wash your feet before dinner so that
Mother would be happy,

Mother, now dead who had gray tears
When you came home alone, lines
Around the mouth darkened when she knew
No one else was coming back.

But you let him take your picture
Because your lettuce is clean now
It has come from a good walled garden
On the edge of the cliff in a good clean village

You shake your lettuce cage dry in the sun
Wave to the men playing boules by the stream
And you think of leeks fat for dinner, potatoes
Dirt groveled chthonic and waiting,

And trout caught in early dawn,
All for your family coming soon, where
Laughter loud from grandchildren will
Surround your table, satisfy a deep longing

In the day's last light, while the sun drops
Behind the wall of gorge, where you can hear
The stream from the village
Fall down into the river endlessly flowing.

Midnight Call from Normandy

For Bobby Beard

I. An army born on shells from the sea

Soldiers fall from nothing into *nada*,
moon-lighting gray beach dunes
down over wave-springs sliding toward dawn

dirt to dust pointing lanes, *bursts in the violet air*
Brécourt Manor, Carentan, 101St Airborne
securing beaches, voices echo like gunshot

over hedgerows, *By our troth we owe God*—
until trees burst like crosses *no one need ever
worry about hell who was there that day*

those days crucified like steeples dictating
soldiers' grace under gunfire: the hanged man
at this cross-roads is voiceless

II. *Quis ut Deus*

Edging the Rock all points the sky: *Quis ut*
Normandy under high blue—wind dry—
clasped hands remember Santiago

hymns in stone towers resurrect saints in dove wings
flashing through arches and pillars like great trees
I think: dried-poppies are never enough

discovered years later in a journal creased
like a worn-out poem—to tell how lamb

graze fast gray tides toward Tombelaine's buried

God of Light, fierce wind speared like sunset
over the serpentine bayshore enclosing Le Mont;
what joy soldiers must have found in Mère Poulard

that year—French girls white bloused mixing eggs
like summer rain, after rising above beaches
living for a green world—*well worth the fighting for*

I make a phone call from a payphone on the Rock,
those of us who know walk very slowly
the rain in the night is cold and I sleep in the streets.

III. "*Resister*: it is our lot, our portion, and our joy."

His feet thread the roads of Normandy rolling
golden wheat fields, pacing the gun-silver channel
waving in rhythms like horses beating earth

he tastes in cold metallic dawn the bite of sea-spray
sips pastis from the hands of peasants—eyes burning
in green-ghost sacrament, echoing midnight calls home

news from afar: *Afghanistan wakes to night
terror, Iran prayer-protests resist tear gas
Neda shot in the head awaits eternal sleep,*

*green-robes silenced like the press omitting death-twitters
of Christians, priests, in China, writers siphoned
to holding-cells for pictures of a bloodied stone square*:

payphones rattle change like ejected shells;
he thinks: why am I not fighting with my brothers;
he hears: after the miracle, all else seems ashes,

and six years in the Marines was long,
here I am a wanderer stooping forgotten roads
where tourists crowd for postcards backpackers

take pictures of lone pilgrim waking on beach sands
tipping the grass above sliding tides: he calls
frantically one last time from the road to Carentan

promises to tell a friend—to bring him back—satisfied
he sets the phone and sees at his feet a scallop shell
etched into a stone tile pointing toward a field of stars.

La Pomme d'Eve

For Andrew Sallee

La Pomme d'Eve meant Eve's Apple
Under the streets of Paris where George
The South African converted a gothic cellar
Into a sports pub, two big screens,
Plenty of Brazilians and Italians and
The only place near the Panthéon
To watch baseball and drink beer

Eve's Apple meant Lucky Strikes, tonight
It meant try your luck on a Parisian blonde
Strike out, swing hard, another beer George
When she came in Barry Bonds was at bat
Andy just in from practice—a coach
For the French national baseball team
And he said, *write a poem today you sad*

Excuse for a Hemingway and I said
Another shut out, no hitter, except for
That one over there, and she smiled
Don't trust Parisian women, he said
All Latina all the way—Andy liked Latinas
He wanted to be a folksinger but he was
From California; then the blonde smiled

My head spinning as she fixed a shoe lace
It was all over for me deep under
The streets of Paris, under the Panthéon
The Temple of Reason left me helpless
The urge to unreason consumed me
I decided to take a bite myself

I moved slow toward her table,

Careful like climbing a strange tree
She tilted into English when I sat down
Lilting each phrase with a breath catch
Finally I had to know
You like baseball I asked *you like*
That guy at bat—she shuddered at
Barry Bonds in HD on the big screen

I have all his rookie cards I said—what an idiot
I thought in the deafening buzz of the TV
I sipped my beer, she stared at her drink
Soon Bonds and his swollen head struck out
I stood, didn't bother to say goodbye
When I walked toward the bar Andy smiled
Ordered another beer—that night

I smoked a whole pack of Lucky Strikes
And resolved to never mention Barry Bonds
To another woman again— perhaps that was like
Original Sin I thought; and maybe
Andy was right—try my luck at Latinas—
At least toward dawn nodding homeward
I could write a poem about a girl named Grace

An Original Sin Image

For T. E. Hulme

I.

Charity we have had, some time in paradise
in the unread rhythms of your voice
where man meets beauty under dug-out:
imagistes in the silence before explosion,

I can see now how a shell buried it
in Amy Lowell, the old moth-eaten
pages of her book, a nothing we know
nothing about
        in chains, tethered to the sound
        of broken fits, welded like an air strip.

But Saint Eloi in his stone-tumbling
towers survives to bless
the horse that dragged the queen across
her realm and between the Devil's stones

goldsmiths affirm the thread
in the pattern—a final judgment
        Giudizio Universale
where one day the arched sky blue
touched canal silver and we rode under
scattered sunlight into "this thy city"
        on bended wave—memoria.

II.

I can sometimes see beside a broken abbey

the figure of a praying man
chanting aloud: "*Grüss Gott . . . the hymn . . .*
    ist gekommen . . ."

He stooped with as much damn near list
as that tower on Burano, colored houses,
we walked the water, bought box wine
late night in the Campo San Stefano—
    we're gonna need the Germans back
someday—and gelato, felt dawn glow
bells in towers, while some working girl
recently recovered from a tuppenny up-right
    sounds like a dime-store piano to me
recalls a momentary mania before
the *coitus interruptus*
    you pay extra
    for that service, that way,
the *jouissance* of *solus ipse* and the
denouement of a used condom until
somebody opened a window
    just to let the air in

then stooping for a loose boot-lace,
I saw tears in her eyes, and I loved her
then knowing somehow
Original Sin kept us all alive together.

III.

Nothing, you implied, is a corridor
in the mind, a violent reflective
absentminded in the consolation
of a six-lined poem:

where we arrive at the discontinuity

between holy water and the
"absolution imparted with certain words"
redeemed only by the asymptotic beauty
of a hand upright moving crosslines in air

for an unknown grief and call to ecstasy—
but known, heard, half-heard
like children playing by the yew tree
or in the bushes where robins no longer weep:
       there is someone whispering
          over a candle perhaps for you too.

IV.

If only we could resurrect some center
       Rousseau:
in your prayers, pray for us, now and at the hour
of your death, even violence too
is romantic even the half-decayed abbey
is photographic for the tourist.

If only we could resurrect some center:
       the rose petals cannot hold
       the poets turn to and fro
       from lines behind sandbag trenches.

If only desultory silence over
the dead horse's belly—
       dead because
       we shot em, bear-bait, crosslines,
       never finished with sorrow—if only
the English had rockets, we might think
about air power some time.

Copernicus—center: Rousseau, ending

things have ends and centers . . .

V.

The figure of a man praying, *dove sta*:
Nada y pues nada in our beginning.

Portraite d'Une Sainte

Blue dusk robes a breaking Notre Dame
Her hands fish a kiss in silver rain

The Slow Deliberate Form of Affection

For Mary de Rachewiltz

> *nothing matters but the quality*
> *of the affection—*
> *in the end—that has carved the trace in the mind*
> *dove sta memoria*
>
> *Ezra Pound, Canto LXXVI*

I.

the barefeet at bottom shining on stone
on stones in the water by San Pantelon
      deep in the junk shop of fresco-forest
      a secret black virgin waits behind altar

I once hid in shadow apse
my hands beheld her altered shadow
      behind trees against Frari
      Mother Nature stooped to folly

but the house has been broken
and I dream each night of Torcello
      cauchemar
      that there is no mortar

what an ugly word *mortar*
coming at you coming and then
      nothing is never all right again;
      they even took Hem's knee cap

and he dreamt of dying
and dreams held him like mortar
      until 1922: to set here the roads

        dust on a rusty blade polished beads

learn how to chisel stones
write poems for people you love
        nothing matters but the quality of country
        and beads smoothed under callused fingers

II.

I know a secret about a girl in a forest
leaning on a broken pillar living song
        the wall is still standing
        and the garden of stone fragments

lie about her,
amid thy quiet house
        no doubt painted on her face
        there are lines in her face

and the lines are hieroglyphic
the heart turns hierophantic
        in the other room words
        "to show" "holy" a hero in arms

III.

I have clipped dried geranium heads
to achieve the probable in the garden
        one day I carried buckets of rocks
        up spiral steps up tower doors

one day I hauled stones to altar
on the summit cross
        when I built the gate on the tower roof
        you said: *something useful*

the mountains are on fire in the night
Sizzo led me toward the light
    voices behind the castle singing in a grove
    the sacred heart of Jesus calls the cuckoo

    nothing is solid: the liquid mountain
    who can trace the sense in this palimpsest

IV.

fire is form: the word is beauty
I failed in breath on the mountaintop
    and the only marble temple erected
    is a word where memory resides

        logos
        eidos (not that word, not yet)

the secret on the mountain is a girl
and the way she herds the goats
    mountain goats blown against the grass
    do not believe in second comings

her secret is a dream and you can call it Time
or raw gravel ground to pieces *contrition*
    down the spiral sunset mountain
    I gaze upon the light until

a dream where points of gold petals
fit together, *the dark pattern is gold*
    the wall stands in a garden
    drafts and fragments

the dome lines form a mother contrapposto
hand gesture cupping child in the pattern

        you can trace the sense: gloom
        cracked in little gold corners

breathing cantos
where the bird's beak dips *cadahus*
        in excelsis your slow deliberate voice
        traces the carven memories

        I lift up my pen to your voice
        I cannot stop hearing your voice in his pages.

Hiking up Mutspitze with Hemingway and Pound

I sat upon Brunnenburg's steps in warm sun
For the gondolas cost too much that June
And there were no guides, just one creased plastic
Map across my knees marking the cross: Mutspitze

When Pound came here in '58 from the hospital
He wanted to erect three columns for his temple
Atop the Mutspitze, an open roof to the heavens
For the rush of sunlight in crystal oblivion

But columns were never built on the mountain-top
And Hemingway never made it to Brunnenburg's rocks
Though he hoped writing late July '58 how he would
Show up soon, praying the "Schlossing is good"

And in that same letter he wrote about feeling
"a little bit Schloss broken" himself, describing
Schnee-Eifel, "sept-oct '44" helping without rank
"illegal and irregular troops . . . a 28 mile open right flank"

Luminous details even 14 years later that haunt
Hemingway's memory, perhaps an apology attempt
Knowing he's gone out too far this time and
Will never see Schloss Brunnenburg or Pound again;

So I started up from the castle to the crucifix
Where red roses climb a shadowed Christ-house
This would be for Pound, Hemingway, and Mary de Rachewiltz—
Pound's daughter—who still wanted columns on Mutspitze

I walked through the Apfelweg's green orcharded rows,

Seeing how Hemingway learned from Pound, to know
Landscape, his homage to Pound and Cézanne in "Big Two-
Hearted River"—even if Ezra thought fishing was a joke,

And the irony that *Fly Fisherman Magazine* printed a sliver
Of Cantos on fishing flies, *Blue dun, number 2 in most rivers*;
The path then slipped under shadow, wafers of light
Cleaving to a form of slopes and criss-crossed sight

Finally under needled light the pine forest walking
A path steady uphill, half-light, not a lost shatter, feeling
My pack shift switchbacks with the weight
Of heavy *Cantos* and *A Moveable Feast*

I remembered Mary's eyes when she told me, "Look,
The only person Hemingway was nice to in that book
Was my father, and that was charity
In the end, we are measured by our generosity"—

I thought Mary was a lot kinder and more Christian
Than me too; maybe she also got that from her father,
She always makes it all cohere, all right; thinking
The quality of affection dictates this walking,

Then the climb over stone steps steepened to Mutkopf
Many passing downward greeting with "Grüss Gott"
Knees brushed steep stone stairs like kneeling before
A shaded crucifix or pilgrims climbing Rocamadour

Then out of darkness you could see it hovering
600 meters to climb in open air, snow iced-over in
Hollows, tinkling bells wave in wind over coarse
Grass, sheep graze the high pass toward the cross

Legs then alone turned before rock scramble

I realized suddenly seeing the distance traveled
How we are only stronger at the broken places after
Having gone out too far and then going farther

I thought of Pound returning from St. Elizabeths
Free but no legal rights, the way Mary said he had
Felt none of his old things belonged to him,
"Tragic heart they have flayed your compassion"

But he still made those drafts, still moments
Of brightness, as he wrote in original fragments,
Beauty exists: "MA LA BELLEZZA ESISTE"
On the true path to paradise—through charity

And Hemingway too, after crashes, never the same
In the eyes, writing toward the end through pain
Drafts and fragments, trying to shore against ruin
The way they've tried to take it all away from him

Those who know read with *infinite love and compassion*
The palimpsest that remains; so over the last rock chasm
On the first high peak above Brunnenburg, I lifted
These thoughts to the high cross, hands shifted

To grasp wood rising from stone, I etched in
The rock three columns, read aloud a section
From *A Moveable Feast*, the old one, then singing
"I'll Fly Away" facing south toward Assisi

I shouted the words for Sparrow and Saint Francis
The world never had a chance to break them
They just climbed a higher mountain I have yet to see,
The verb, as Pound wrote, "see," not "walk on," yet

I read then from Canto CXVI, about that Terzo, around

Third Heaven, where maybe Hemingway and Pound
Finally met to talk about Venere, Venus,
About Schlossing with Dante and Villon

It coheres all right, once you've climbed on through
Beyond the stopping point you learn how to excuse
Hemingway's Hell and Pound's Paradiso,
The green world and our inheritance remains;

It was time to descend then with sun glare
Make it down before dark, down long stairs,
Knees jolting greeting even square-eyed goats
Along the path with a cheerful "Grüss *Goat*"

Past the guest house on Mutkopf through sun slant
Bird songs traced the crooked path into dark descent
Finally village lights around the church glowed the hollow
Where waters dictated a path to the Castle at the Well

Then home with a little light by the moon, here
I try to write these notes, to make the day cohere
Do not speak, I think, let the wind on Mutspitze speak now
And light a candle in the temple for Hemingway and Pound.

La Route de Cacharel:
An Appeal to Richard Aldington

For Catherine Aldington

I.

I saw your daughter moving for joy
Her laughter against sunlight:
She forgot herself in smiling sun
When the arched stones of Glanum
Met like crooked pilgrim staffs
The blue sky carving Les Alpilles
Into slopes for olive groves.

After Jacques Moniquet, *il miglior fabbro*
Bijoux en argent, and the Saint Estelle
He placed in the palm of my hand,
Bid us almonds and afternoon farewell,
I talked of Estella, *le pèlerinage*, and the
Coquille Saint-Jacques hung from my neck,
We shouted to stones: "Liber Sancti Jacobi!"

Later we drove past the Val d'Enfer
And laughed at finding ourselves
Per una selva oscura, until we came to
Montmajour and Lucien Clergue's exhibition
And how he almost told me once
Something about transposed nude bullfighters
And the mystery of Hemingway's *toreo* . . .

The wind was right that day combing *romarin*
And the *sauge* we picked from above
Arles seasoned our *poulet fermier* from the market

She drank Heinekens from a cooler
And we sang Johnny Cash songs together
Until we descended into the Camargue
And the straight wind always dictated the road then.

II.

There had always been Saint-Guilhem
Then of course the Cours Mirabeau where
We held our hands under moss fountain
And danced a waltz for the Good King—
She made me wander to the church
Waited and then bought me a pipe. We talked
About writing, and we decided I should go home

And finish my degree with Stoney
That I would always have a room at
Mas "Les Pellegrins" and the typewriter
Would be waiting. But most of all, she said,
I should go back to help Sparrow
And to plant their garden, learn about
Poireaux and the joy of growing things.

III.

I write this to you Mr. Aldington
As one might pray for intercession to a saint
Not that either of us are saintly
Nor that we should be discussing sanctity
This late at night, but the agony, as you wrote,
Of grief and pity—or sorrow at the distance—
Compels me to supplication:

That I have walked some of The Way, surely,
And that I ended where I began, with Catha

Your daughter, *oui, Monsieur*: so,
Wherever you are, I supplicate on her behalf
Because I'm afraid the sound of my typewriter
Is too far away for her to hear—I can
Remember the joy you enflamed in her

The way she wanted to sing when I read your
Poems aloud to her; her smile and eyes that
Made men fall in love with her; of course,
In the Camargue I am sure that worried you—
When she told me, "Never stop writing,
See and write always,"
I thought of you and life for life's sake

Soon I learned how it made her happy
To hear the sound of the typewriter in mornings
The way pounding keys reminded her
Of you, so I wrote every day
Even when I had nothing to say
It brought you back, a momentary release
From time, it was then I knew you would write

One more poem, that you would come back
With pilgrim staff in hand and we might meet
Somewhere on the route to Cacharel
Where garganey gather nightly, and the poachers
In *les étangs* eye by Church-light the wing-flash
And take to mother enough for caban-fare,
At least, you might catch the Light Show

Of Aubanel's *La Bête du Vaccarès*
And find, again, history's facts contradicting
Fiction's farewell; or some flamingoes, at least:
Either way, we can both ride white horses to her
Rescue between *Lou Biòu* and the *cloche*

Sounding like a death bell in the fields rocking
Beyond the canals and wind-crossed reeds.

IV.

One day my horse wandered into the marshes
Far from the herd, from the *gardians* calling
   allez allez allez
One day I wandered bewildered in the Camargue
And my horse—his name was Wagner—
Started galloping: I held on tight—a poor fool
Water splashed knees over boots, faster
He found the path tamarisk trees slapping

He kept going faster and faster I held tighter
But then heaving gallop: I felt I was flying
And rode the wind and yellow sun—
Suddenly as we drew up to the bulls
And the *gardians*, I wanted to sing:
  Chevalier de la table ronde . . .
  Will the circle be unbroken . . .
I missed singing certain songs with friends
The complicity of voices harmonizing distance—

The dark Camargue is an isolation of spirit,
Where mistral winds blow sand through windows
Huddled at my empty shoes; I found alone
It was her laughter aloud against the night
That taught me something about bearing love
And holding tight against lonesomeness
To laugh away the dark when night descends.

Poem for Denys Colomb de Daunant: Though I Never Met Him

For Eric Forbeaux

somewhere on the route to Cacharel
was a man, Denys Colomb de Daunant
I never met him nor stayed at his *Mas*
but I've seen the masterpiece *Crin Blanc*

the way the bright savage sun compels
our rage to tame the wild beast and calm
the burning heart inside our cage of flesh
walking dreams on water under sun

one night late after watching *Crin Blanc*
I felt the urge to walk into the sea
wandered down along Le Petit-Rhône
until I found the tomb of Baroncelli

"Folco" I cried across the *sansouïre*
the moon a crescent curve of horns
a bell clang stumbled in the marsh's glare
a black bull led the dark, the *simbèu*

the boy Folco in *Crin Blanc* finds
endless seas and white crested waves
the poet Folco de Baroncelli
wrote about the bull to Montherlant

Lou Biòu leaping black in sea dance
the awesome urge of danger, an endless dark;
the Camargue reveals the depth of a man
his fears, the way he breaks when rage consumes

his ordinary heart, the way he yearns
beyond himself for something else to love
or just to hold in darkness until he hears
birds alighting an island far away—

the Camargue where the white horse
and black bull shape the sand stricken church
where somewhere on the route to Cacharel
a man discovered how to live his dream

we are compelled to frame this strange joy
setting words to horses catching light
as *gardians* hold steady against the bull
to capture God in birds along the shore

        we sing the wind in mourning with the sea
        we live the wedded song of sky and sand

II

Nekuia: Calling the Still Small Voice

Salut, salut,
O Saintes Maries!

I. Roncevaux

Ah that wind breathes thick
in the throat like a ringing thrush
beech wood turning brown spots

rock and root is a hymn worn path
feet deep upward from the stone cross
christened by sun shafts shaking

I am not a pilgrim but I have a passport
to Mass it is the first I have attended in years
I cannot remember how long:

after praying for everyone I can think of
I find before me a silver virgin framed blue
I bow in sudden soul eclipse

but her face holds transient light
before broken glass, *Nuestra Señora*
I cannot remember if I am supposed to believe

in prayers, I cannot stop praying:
I am not a pilgrim I say aloud to myself
I ascend the mountain alone to myself

in the mountains are bells
and the smooth slopes steep in woods
are blank and bare until forest and beech wood

and Charlemagne's horse beyond
beyond the fog: Roland his name rhymes
with Odysseus, Penelope replaced by Mary

ah, the fog still spells his name and the empty
hooks on his stone await the singing of some
divine comedy in the chastity of time unforgiven

my knees find the grass, the worn world is old
yet my passport—*carnet de pèlerin de saint-jacques*—
tells me forty-three kilometers to Pamplona

long long the road bulls and sun and shadow
shut out of the pilgrim's hostel after 10pm
no admittance—dancing down the street

riau riau colors her colors and hair swirling
giants marching on the square later a room
in La Perla by luck: who is this lady on my arm,

I never told her my name: *sol y sombra*
long long the climb I will always remember
the climb out of the bowl

of hills around Pamplona high high
I am not a pilgrim: until then in Puenta la Reina
on the Calle de Crucifijo, a chapel of stone

her voice compelled me to kneel before the Y-cross
knowing: I will make Santiago de Compostela
by July 25 2004 I will kiss the bishop's ring

I will yearn beyond the sun for the end of faith
and find in the end the endurance of stone—made
possible only by the discovery of incense

Botafumeiro—and Saint James' bejewelled mantle
or maybe just some mysterious transfiguration
climbing on through the Pass of Roland

II. Saint-Guilhem-le-Désert

The ruined castle is a temple of Time
only a fortress really: the Château du Géant
where the short nosed warrior defeated
the Giant Saracen in time forgotten
        on the ridge crown rocks are full of nests
        thyme and the gray sky.

I see it high from the road after crossing
Pont du Diable and the howling grotto—
Grotte de Clamouse a cry shivers my bones
I cannot explain sorrow but there is sound
        a mother's grief when she found
        her son's body in water—

the path through the village is stone.
I am rapt in rain watching water cut stones;
below the church is a fountain
eau potable says the scallop shell
        drink deep deeper than water
        eyes channel rain and light.

In the church I stand before a piece of wood
what I am told is from the True Cross;
I do not know what to believe, I do not
know why I am along the via Tolosana
        the east west route stretching—
        I begin between two endings.

Outside the church: arches and apses
above I climb the cliffs clutching roots
mud rock slick below is a long fall
and gravel slides under feet until
        ahead the broken arch the summit

        I find the saint standing alone;

he is tall in the archway of the broken castle.
I stumble disjunct eyes rise to see him
he smiles as I falter for words
whelmed on top of the world
        a violation trespass if you will
        on the ancient domain of Time.

He seems a carven image until he lifts a
sword toward sky rain glistens a rosary,
there are no words to answer exile
though the search has brought me here
        and what am I but a wretch
        on the edge of the abyss—

the sky bends to his hand
he whispers so low I cannot hear
in the sudden wind the shape of his voice
then light flash and thunder he is gone
        I finger the soaked bread
        cross cold in my pocket;

perhaps never there I think: until at my feet
roll colored beads. I take these and climb down
toward the church the path curving inward
an edge like the scallop shell pointing the church;
        I know when I find the plane tree—
        it is a True Cross shard

tempered in the locked cross-case
a covenant contained beyond crown or crow
Charlemagne's gift to his cousin Guilhem
a temple untouched by time
        demanding not less than everything
        a charity I may never be worthy to name.

III. Sainte-Baume

High up in the forest is a holy cave
there are giant stone steps carved in earth
fashioned for greater men before time
became the slow drip drop of rain
down twisted beech branches, the forest
is haunted and the holy cave is high,

above the grotto angels can be seen
on the mountaintop seven times daily
and with them a woman singing
in a strange tongue, her robe whirling light
about the summit so that at certain hours
her body forgets itself laughing with angels,

I have seen it so I swear in late January once
after morning rain, the climb was slow moss
dripping a strange northern forest in that
Mediterranean air like at Roncevaux where
roads turn in Pyrenees fog, but this was Provence and
Mary Magdalene never needed an Olifant;

still I felt Roland's spirit walked among these trees
chanting some chastity song to Our Lady while
Charlemagne bathed in a spring away in sunlight
attended to by his light and long haired lady-lovers;
yet the stone stairs did not speak their names
above the forest I found the door high in the sky—

the Massif de la Sainte-Baume above Saint-Maximin
where only hours before I trembled rapt in darkness
held by her bones beneath the altar; why are we
compelled to find holy places in mountains to climb
up from the dark caverns of soul—is climbing a form

of expiation, is seeking the virgin dark an act of love—

inside her grotto was dark and damp the floor was water
I took off my boots followed the stream to the springs
candlelight glistened beneath my feet,
her stone figure waving in shadow and light
I had come to seek refuge from fire, the bright blaze
of unholy love my heart a burning cauldron

I wanted to say aloud inside the silent cave
rescue me, my Lady from the tumult of flesh, carry me
to the summit beyond my burning thirsting dream.
Then without pause I fell in love with the shape
of her bust, feeling ridiculous—it was merely a statue
or was it and was I aching to have her in my arms

her long hair down my back like wind or waves
wheeling in the dark on the moist stone slab
fire to fire my soul dancing with Mary Magdalene—
suddenly the door to the grotto opened light
angled over the wet floor of the cave
and a dozen people filed in cameras pointing

flashes and beeping noises I hid behind her stone
until one, a young woman, edged away from the group
knelt in the stream of the spring holding hands
she wept; I watched as water pooled around her
a flooding feeling in my throat, tears spilled
I began uncontrollably to weep with her

I wanted to touch her face, trace the lines of her eyes
to hold her tight very tight shaking she was shaking
and I could not stop crying with her remembering
my own broken words a resurrection of betrayals
and the smell gone from the indent in the pillow

after the long long morning wakes like winter—

I did not know myself in the shadows of the grotto
then she stood and left and the water left no imprint
and the only image I have of her is there kneeling
beside Mary Magdalene in the spring cave
where she reminded me of a feeling like forgiveness
and the way stone holds the light of darkness

        pooled under the spring cracked lines that follow
        inward the scrutiny of a faded scallop shell

IV. Les Saintes-Maries-de-la-Mer

the wind on the plain of Camargue makes the sunrise
flame and burn the horses a white fire blazing

the morning is cold and I need to make a fire
she does not moan for morning yet the sun

in zero stillness light moves above a mound of sand
its horns curve the line of earth away

after fire wakes the house I ride toward the sea
starting egrets in meadows until bells make the tower

a swollen magpie bows along the crossing road
stumbling into sand and hoof marks

the hymn *Provençau e Catouli*
curves the banks along Le Petit-Rhône

until seas wash beach-wood smooth wash German bunkers
even tourists forget for a moment between the marshes

but that night far out in the marais and the way the wind
the way the dog held fast fast faster skin tight against your leg
the way the wind moved the boat the long pole pushing
the way the dog watched him push the boat as you held tight
to the wind and the last fading light of day the last of the day
became a moveable star field and the first of the night was
light radiant around the church beyond beyond the swamp
and suddenly he said quiet dont move let the gun speak
suddenly in the fading sun rising firing a burst and far a splash
dont move dont shift doucement douce douce
and the dog shivered not for the cold but for the—and another
rising steel brought the churchlight to black sky

*bursting with fire in the deepening dark and the crack not splash
on an ice sheet far out in mistral wind waiting waiting
waiting for the silhouette of the church to move like a fortress
defending the sky waiting for the maries to return on their boat
waiting for the end of anguish that begins in the night
and finds in the unforgettable darkness that you are only yourself
suddenly a flash without burst just the fire and the sound far
he set out decoys then and the dog leapt into water and after
a nameless time returned with three birds colored one still alive
three and one alive and he took his neck and let me hold it
and I lost myself holding the little bird of the marshes
small and in my hands cacharel and the decoys floated out
and again he the burst and the night was on fire and I the fire
he hands me an empty shotgun shell a souvenir he says in the dark
contending with time and the time wore on and beyond always
the light glowed around the church of the saintes maries
and later around midnight we pushed back through marshes
the dog satisfied and panting against my belly
the pole found the underwater stiff and freezing
and we chained the boat to a sand mooring and found the path in
moon light and then the truck and I placed the half-dozen
birds in the backseat and later that week after plucking
would eat better than I ever had my whole life and still ever*

high above the town the church steps spiral
the stone roof tiles scale the line of blue

the bullring a small circle the gypsies do not sing
the church of Les Saintes-Maries is not a mountain

but I can see down the coast Sainte-Baume and away
far the Cévennes, Pic Saint-Loup

and beyond the road, the route, *la route . . . camino*
the church is not a mountain but I have climbed it long

there is no one on the rooftop
until she walks along the edge around the chapel

her hair with gold flecks and eyes like the sea
she has come over the sea and sun

she sings for her lost boy who was given a pillar
of jasper from Our Lady dressed in the colors of heaven

and later discovered the ends of the earth
then by grace—his body killed by Herod 44 A.D.—

was translated along the field of stars, the *campus
stellae*, where years later the French Knight drowning was

brought ashore covered in cockle shells the man
who saved him smiled like a peasant or ancient fisherman

I am Santiago but you can call me Saint-Jacques
the Patron of Spain is always the Glory of France

I see all of this in a vision from her song that fills the air
I walk toward her on the edge of the church roof

feet slip falling and she reaches for my hand
her grip holds me reminds me of stone—

the Tree of Jesse in the Portico of Glory—
I am lost in Saint Mary Salome's beauty

my heart drops until I climb back onto the roof
when I stand to look at her she is gone

and in my hand is a small sea-washed shell
my fingers hold the shell climbing down the church

suddenly horses and bulls rush the streets
there are children gathering beyond the village

for a morning *ferrade* just a minor *fête*
in the distant bluegray morning

along the route to Cacharel
I watch and laugh I am the only English speaking

drinking their wine they smile pastis and whiskey
they hand me brie and bacon and baguette

and tell me to catch the bull's horns he is charging
the ground shakes my hands find his horns

I run with him and then heels scrape sand turning
I twist his crown of thorns and over my body—

falling together we fall as one
four men hold him down with me the brand on fire

he stares and I am suddenly aware
of something else as if for the first time

his eye is the color of jasper I am no longer alone
my body heavy against his shoulder

flesh twitches with fire I feel the shell in my pocket
as I ease away and he jumps free running

after the smell of burning hair morning church bells
are so distant nobody knows how long they toll

Coda—Le Pèlerinage:
Les Saintes-Maries-de-la-Mer

I hold her hand as waves wash over our feet
singing loud *Salut, salut, O Saintes Maries*
her eyes sing aloud the depths of the sea

dark gypsy hands reach up the boat is high
gray eyes chant—*Vive Les Saintes Maries
Vive La Sainte Sara*—waves lift us to sky

she dances in water weaving light
we reach for the boat and touch fingers
her voice edges the sky around the saints

we look at each other say nothing waves
lap our bodies and sand is in our hair away
bishop robes over dunes *gardians* trot out the day

procession vanishes into carnival a man ratchets
a hurdy gurdy *you picked a fine time to leave me*
suddenly we are not alone we see familiar faces

though we do not name them gliding beside
compound of sea and sand eyes like a friend
or some long lost mother for whom we cried

we step infinite and slow until a fish leaps
into the chaos of sun windless over a wide sea;
we sing harmony on forgotten beaches

with voices out of the irredeemable past present
only in hymns over water and the steady vibration
of hearts together mounting wind over sand

III

Not Just *La Patria*—For RPW

For West is where we all plan to go some day. It is where you go when the land gives out and the old-field pines encroach.
       Robert Penn Warren

Walking out of Notre Dame there beyond
The pigeons Charlemagne, Roland, and Olivier
Face the west lingering like ghosts brackened
Green on the edge above that aged bronzed river:
This will be my final night in Paris alone
Before I move south for the winter.

I look across to the Left Bank, Shakespeare & Co.
Remembering the nights reading Warren's
A Place to Come To upstairs on a sagging bed
Dusty beside a window facing Notre Dame;
Warren brought the earth, *la terra*, into focus
Made the past edge fiercely over tomorrow;

I had fled to France, to escape the maelstrom
The vision-curse of American western solitude
"Go west, my son," and lose yourself into sublime
Emptiness, a delight in mere survival, selfhood,
Thinking this, I was startled when overhead
I heard cathedral bells rolling time into clouds;

Charlemagne, that legend of the Western World,
Hovered with staff ready to strike down
The enemies of the West: where was Roland's
Horn, where were the pine trees and the breath
That long blew our past into forgetfulness
Ah que ce cor, he said long ago, but the battle

Is never won and the soul contends for amnesty
In the epic of our ancestry: do we return to
Roncevaux and find, as if for the first time,
The immutability of stone rising from earth
Do we sing lost songs in crowded brasseries
Over a mug of Mutzig and cassoulet because

We are unable to resign ourselves to the end
Of what we love, because we, like the stone,
Will not fall down to the terror of the times—
We inherit from the dead more than a history:
The direction of a hand gesture dripping water,
The discovery of self in the gloom of landscape

In the doom of a strange land; we inherit voices
The dead speak if we listen, but how do we hear
Them in the cackling of the modern world—
At dawn, the train departs Paris, land unfolds southward
The sea shimmers soon beyond Avignon, ruins
Thinking, *nothing is lost, nothing is ever lost.*

Notes for the Last Waltz

For Dino, Catha's grandson

I.

She told me,
     you don't have to leave
you can stay, your room is made up,
we have everything you need,

and you have the machine à écrire
a basic statement with well-wrought
manners holding tight to facts—she was
always factual in her manners, though

passionate in her outbursts, and
the outbursts were plenty, mostly laughter.
And look, with you here now I am
painting, I have not painted since

well, in years,
     I told her I was in love, I
tried to change the subject, wanted
her to know I found something she

would understand, would justify
my having to leave again, something
anything to keep from seeing her
daughters cry as I walked away;

I believe you but you remember what
the Camargue does to us, stricken
I knew what she meant and had always

balanced the knowing with the longing

and facts with manners—
we laughed about all this once,
the way hearts break away like
a fairy-tale, some far-away land where

the castle turret lady sings the sun
while dragons threaten the skyline.
But suddenly her grandson ran in
waving a broomstick at me, holding

the lid of a pot, *Dragon! Dragon!*
he screamed, ready to slay some
evil spirit crouching toward home
Dino, my, I am an old woman,

and I grabbed him, lifted skyward,
he whirled with belly laughter;
I threw him on her bed, and she
gasped and roared a smile and

leapt up to my arms, clutching
and we waltzed a short step
and Dino joined us and we held
each other until the end of time.

II.

You hear the bell of the *simbèu*
who knows where it wanders
it is carried far far over the *marais*
in this wind tonight—

I am not a *gardian* of bulls,

but I will try to guard your words
in a poem etched clear like
sun shaping the edge of *salicorn*

distant pines and pointing cypress
I will hold your poem close
like an egret's wings to windward
until the last dance

when we all gather together
beyond the western seas
and hold tight to actuality
to the hope that transcends possibility.

Waiting for Beatrice in the Alyscamps

It was not for nothing that Dante thought of the Aliscamps in his Inferno.
                              Ezra Pound

the alley of poplar trees tunnels the sparrow's
flight hard stone to ground wings, first
you saw the dust burst orange: *lou soulèu*
we shouted; sparrows scattered raised the soles
of pilgrims kneeling at picnics and prayers

by marble tombs we chanted: *me fai canta*
the fine eye sings for me and wings flash
flutter drop and hover beak stashed crumbs
piled by a stained cork under an almond
tree; blue beckons the sky narrow

light enough to read in shades the *chanson*
of Roland's fall, ghosts linger here where
it was said his army lay buried crossed
now under bird claw hieroglyphs in dust
you should have put that in your cantos

you probably did and we don't remember
and Dante knew it was not about the horn
that broke nor the ambush nor the sword
but the Lady looking from afar
the day that Roland died at Roncevaux

and her name that we cannot pronounce
arrests even the smallest child running
under the sun, so we wait like Dante in Arles
hesitate until you tell me you've been far

along this road before, point the distance

say, *Van Gogh missed the detail where
cold hands grip a penny coin for Charon
to barter a river ride*—"barter" your word—
beyond the art in eyes of St. Trophime
I say *Elysium arrives in autumn hours*

we wait a long time to see, we stare
alone for a long time and walking closer
a figure passes toward the river rising
I say her name but it sounds like Marie
you only hear the birds' *paradiso*

behind us we do not witness her sitting
beside a man who drops a rose over
her knee and offers a bottle of wine
for we are caught in unstopped time, the siren-
song beatified: we keep on singing—

Eau d'Eden: Farewell to Cacharel
[or The Smell of Cacharel]

For HRS, fellow pilgrim and guide

I've always loved the way the road rides
out from Les Saintes-Maries past horses
hazy eyed in sun stare and black flies
the hanging salt smell of marsh wind
until suddenly the village ends, the road
ahead a ribbon tracing marshes low water
pink hooks on stick legs jolting into wings
as hundreds of flamingoes step into flight
across the vast purple distance of Camargue
I told a friend that I wanted to use the name

of the route as a title to a book of poems,
The Route to Cacharel, I said as we drove.
I slowed by a dirt road, pulled off
and the friend said to me, "that will make
quite an interesting book. I don't suppose
the Camarguaise will mind it, but most others
might think it a little odd. Unless you mean
to write about the road to a perfume and
clothing store, maybe some designer
cowboys can dot your Camargue route."

Puzzled I watched an egret. He said,
"Cacharel is the name of a famous clothes
and perfume label. The designer named it
after the local duck, *cacharel* or
sarcelle d'été, you know, like the one
Robert showed you." He smiled
and I started to laugh at my own romantic

notions of names and places, of roads
smells, the flying of ducks across skies
my own canard-vision gone awry.

"Maybe you can sell your book with
patches of cloth attached as bookmarks
perfumed pages with *Eau d'Eden* by
Cacharel, or maybe one of those supermodels
Gisele Bündchen or even Laetitia Casta
on the cover of your book."
"Yes," I said. "It must be Casta, riding
bareback, she is French—it might sell."
The *marais* was still, the water of Eden
I thought, the smell of the marshes

suddenly two storks arrow winged soared
above reeds white and black. "See them,"
yes I thought, "and their wings." I said,
"they fly like arrowheads in the sky."
"They sometimes return from Africa," he said,
"with arrows in them, they are Pfeilstorch."
I loved to say *cigogne*, stork, in French.
"Maybe those two will make their way
to Strasbourg find the north tower stones
nest in the cathedral my ancestors built."

"Maybe their names are Erwin and Sabina,"
I said. He smiled, the road curved ahead
a sandy lane pocked by rain, horse hooves,
framed by reeds water-light everywhere.
"This really is a garden of Eden," I said.
"Hemingway knew that, Durrell, Van Gogh."
He said nothing. The sky turned ash and pink
behind us the church stones were etched white,
stones buried as deep into earth as high

as they reach into sky, a fortress around the spring

of Mary Salome and Mary Jacobe locked in
the smell of stones, the taste of tarnished brass
I realize all the pilgrimages he has led me
are centered on springs, channeled water.
"This is a good road but we should get back—
long drive tomorrow." I turned the car around
we drove toward village lights, horses in stalls.
"Yes, I'm ready to leave, more roads, new smells,
even the storks don't stay long, passing through."
"All gardens end with Original Sin," he said.

I laughed, "and perfumed pages and bookmarks."
We drove through the village ever-expanding
construction machines new hotels apartments
noise into night, a busload of Germans on bikes
lined the street in front of us, cameras everywhere.
"And tourism always poisons the well."
In the back seat she sat quiet all day watching
the land pass, loving the salt smell and sea birds;
finally she said to our friend, "promise
someday you'll take us to Strasbourg."

www.ingramcontent.com/pod-product-compliance
Lightning Source LLC
Chambersburg PA
CBHW071755080526
44588CB00013B/2243